D1031772

TOTALLY INTO FISHING AND HUNTING

DEER HUNTING

ABBY BADACH DOYLE

 Gareth Stevens
PUBLISHING

Please visit our website, www.garethstevens.com. For a free color catalog of all our high-quality books, call toll free 1-800-542-2595 or fax 1-877-542-2596.

Library of Congress Cataloging-in-Publication Data

Names: Doyle, Abby Badach, author.
Title: Deer hunting / Abby Badach Doyle.
Description: New York : Gareth Stevens Publishing, [2023] | Series: Totally
    into fishing and hunting | Includes index.
Identifiers: LCCN 2022001998 (print) | LCCN 2022001999 (ebook) | ISBN
    9781538280003 (set) | ISBN 9781538280010 (library binding) | ISBN
    9781538279991 (paperback) | ISBN 9781538280027 (ebook)
Subjects: LCSH: Deer hunting–Juvenile literature.
Classification: LCC SK301 .D69 2023 (print) | LCC SK301 (ebook) | DDC
    799.2/765–dc23/eng/20220121
LC record available at https://lccn.loc.gov/2022001998
LC ebook record available at https://lccn.loc.gov/2022001999

Portions of this work were originally authored by Shelby Moran and published as *We're Going Deer Hunting*. All new material in this edition is authored by Abby Badach Doyle.

Published in 2023 by
Gareth Stevens Publishing
29 East 21st Street
New York, NY 10010

Editor: Abby Badach Doyle
Designer: Michael Flynn

Photo credits: Cover, pp. 1, 15 Tom Reichner/Shutterstock.com; series background (camo) Alexvectors/Shutterstock.com; p. 5 Rich Waite/Shutterstock.com; p. 7 Bruce MacQueen/Shutterstock.com; p. 8 Jeffrey B. Banke/Shutterstock.com; p. 9 Rodney Kane Bertola/Shutterstock.com; p. 10 Paul Tessier/Shutterstock.com; p. 11 J Edwards Photography/Shutterstock.com; p. 13 Andy445/iStock; p. 16 Krasula/Shutterstock.com; p. 17 Tony Campbell/Shutterstock.com; p. 19 Neil Podoll/Shutterstock.com; p. 20 FooTToo/Shutterstock.com; p. 21 Jeffrey B. Banke/Shutterstock.com; p. 22 Robert Nyholm/Shutterstock.com; p. 23 Jim Cumming/Shutterstock.com; p. 25 Amee Cross/Shutterstock.com; p. 27 Steve Oehlenschlager/Shutterstock.com; p. 29 stockcreations/Shutterstock.com.

Printed in the United States of America

A NOTE TO READERS
Always talk with a parent or teacher before proceeding with any of the activities found in this book. Some activities require adult supervision.

A NOTE TO PARENTS AND TEACHERS
This book was written to be informative and entertaining. Some of the activities in this book require adult supervision. Please talk with your child or student before allowing them to proceed with any hunting activities. The author and publisher specifically disclaim any liability for injury or damages that may result from use of information in this book.

Some of the images in this book illustrate individuals who are models. The depictions do not imply actual situations or events.

CPSIA compliance information: Batch #CSGS23: For further information contact Gareth Stevens, New York, New York at 1-800-542-2595.

Find us on

CONTENTS

Join the Herd 4

All About Antlers 6

Kinds of Deer 8

Where to Go 10

Be Seen.. 12

Deer Can Sense Danger 14

Rifle or Shotgun? 16

Bowhunting.. 18

Stay Still 20

On the Move.. 22

Ready to Hunt.. 24

Got One!... 26

All in Balance 28

Glossary... 30

For More Information 31

Index.. 32

WORDS IN THE GLOSSARY APPEAR IN BOLD TYPE THE
FIRST TIME THEY ARE USED IN THE TEXT.

JOIN THE HERD

If you haven't gone deer hunting yourself, you probably know someone who has. Every year, millions of people hunt deer in the United States. In fact, deer are the most commonly hunted animal in North America.

You can find deer in large numbers all over the United States. But that doesn't make it any easier to shoot one! Deer run fast and have a sharp sense of smell. If they spot you, they'll run. That's why deer hunters love the **challenge**.

KNOW THE FACTS!

Many Native Americans value deer. Just one animal can provide a lot of meat. Deer can also provide skin and fur to make clothing and shelter. Their bones were used to make tools in the past.

Male deer grow antlers, which are made of bone.

ALL ABOUT ANTLERS

Deer are part of the animal family that includes elk, caribou, and moose. The males of this family all have antlers. Unlike horns, which last a lifetime, antlers fall off in winter or early spring. Male deer grow new antlers each year.

Antlers make great **trophies**. Hunters call antlers "racks." When hunters talk about "points" they mean the tip of each antler branch that's more than 1 inch (2.5 cm) long. A buck with lots of points will impress, or catch the interest of, other hunters!

KNOW THE FACTS!

A fuzzy coating called velvet protects, or guards, the buck's soft antlers as they grow. Velvet falls off in late summer or early fall. Sometimes bucks rub their antlers on trees to help remove it.

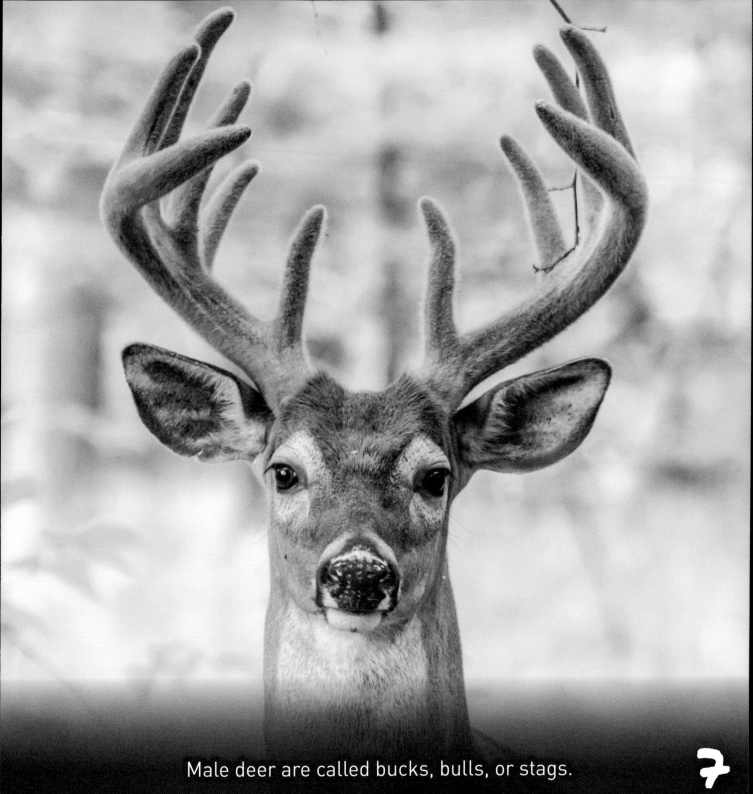

Male deer are called bucks, bulls, or stags.

KINDS OF DEER

The two most common kinds of deer are the white-tailed deer and the mule deer. Whitetails live in just about every U.S. state, except Hawaii and some parts of the Southwest. Whitetails usually weigh between 80 and 200 pounds (36.3 to 90.7 kg).

KNOW THE FACTS!

Black-tailed deer are a type of mule deer. They can be found in northern California, Oregon, Washington, and western Canada.

BLACK-TAILED DEER

You might hear hunters call mule deer "muleys."

Mule deer live in western states, such as Colorado. They can weigh up to 300 pounds (136.1 kg). If you shoot a mule deer or a whitetail, you might need some help dragging it out of the woods!

9

WHERE TO GO

You can hunt in many different places. Deer can be found in forests, fields, swamps, and farm country. Many people prefer hunting in the woods because they can hide in the trees. In hot weather, deer hide in the forest or near water to stay cool.

Hunters call the time just after sunrise and right before sunset the "magic hours."

Deer are most active around sunrise and sunset. It's a smart idea to be in your deer-hunting spot before the sun is up. It takes time for your eyes to **adjust** to seeing in low light.

KNOW THE FACTS!

If you're hunting in low light, be careful when you aim. You want to be able to see the deer clearly to get a good shot! Keeping the rising or setting sun behind your back may help.

BE SEEN

Most states require hunters to wear bright orange so other hunters can see them. Deer can't see this color, but humans can. Deer can see some colors, such as blue. Hunters also often wear **camouflage** clothing that has dull grays and browns to blend in.

Some states have **archery** seasons where you don't have to wear orange. However, this is usually only allowed when deer season doesn't overlap with others, such as turkey season. That's because turkey hunters might be using guns!

KNOW THE FACTS!

Deer are red-green color-blind. To a deer, the color orange looks brown or gray. However, they can spot movement very well.

Bright orange is also called hunter orange or blaze orange. Hunters wear it for their safety so other hunters don't mistake them for deer!

13

DEER CAN SENSE DANGER

Deer have great **defenses**. They have excellent senses of hearing and smell. They're big, but they can run very fast. Once their senses warn them of danger, they can be very hard to catch. Having the right **weapon** is important to bag, or kill, a deer.

Many deer hunters use rifles. These are long firearms, or guns, that are held tightly against the shoulder. Rifles fire long, thin bullets that travel far and cause great harm to their targets.

KNOW THE FACTS!

A deer's sense of smell is much better than a human's. People have five million scent receptors, or receivers. Deer have 297 million!

How Deer Avoid Harm

ears can twist one at a time to follow sounds

great at seeing in low light and spotting movement

tail movement warns other deer of danger

superstrong sense of smell

fast runners and high jumpers

15

RIFLE OR SHOTGUN?

Rifles might be the most popular type of gun with deer hunters. However, they're not the only choice. Some states don't allow certain kinds of rifles. Other hunters prefer a different type of gun.

RIFLE

KNOW THE FACTS!

A scope is a lens on your gun to help you see faraway objects close up.

Good hunters aim for a clean kill without making the deer suffer.

Shotguns scatter small pellets, or beads, called shot. For deer hunting, you can also load shotguns with single shells called slugs. Slugs don't travel far, but they can do a lot of harm. Slugs can kill a deer, while shot often wounds it. It's best to avoid bullets, slugs, or shot made of lead, as it is harmful to other animals.

17

BOWHUNTING

For a greater challenge, some deer hunters choose to hunt with bows and arrows. This is called archery. Archery is one of the oldest forms of hunting. Newer bows, such as **compound** bows, can shoot farther and better than the simple ones used in the past.

Even with these new bows, archery is not easy. Bowhunters must get closer to deer than hunters using rifles and shotguns. They rely on moving slowly and using their sight and hearing to get close without scaring the deer.

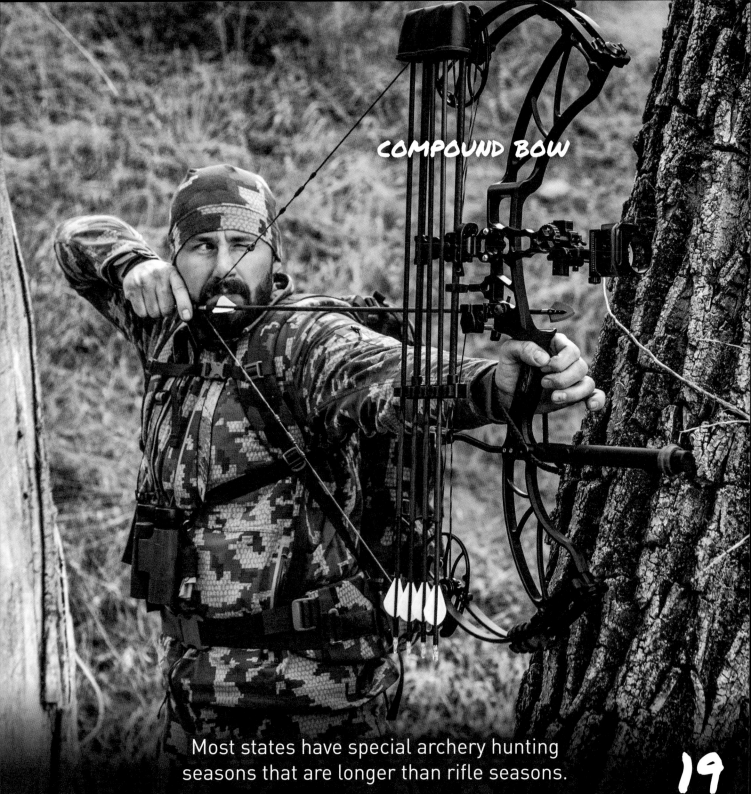

COMPOUND BOW

Most states have special archery hunting seasons that are longer than rifle seasons.

19

STAY STILL

No matter which method you use to hunt, you have to be as quiet as possible. One hunting method is to find a good spot and sit there patiently. Patient means able to stay calm while waiting. A good spot has deer tracks and game trails.

Some hunters sit in tree stands, which are small decks in or near trees. They offer good views of the area. Hunters often hunt with blinds, or screens that hide them from deer.

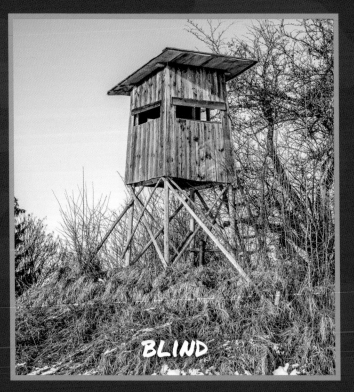
BLIND

For safety, wear a full-body harness when in a tree stand. A harness has straps that connect you to something stable.

21

THE MOVE

Not all hunters sit and wait. Some deer hunters would rather be more active. When stalking, you spot a deer first. Then you move slowly, carefully, and quietly through the woods to get your shot. Stalking requires hunters to pay attention to their surroundings.

KNOW THE FACTS!

Still hunting is similar to stalking. When still hunting, you move quietly until you find a deer, often stopping to stay still and look for deer. When you spot one, you quickly take your shot.

When stalking, even the noise from your clothing might scare the deer.

When stalking deer, hunters keep their eyes open for animal tracks. Snow can play an important role in hunting. Animal tracks can be easy to see in the snow, but a fresh snowfall will hide them.

READY TO HUNT

Before your first hunt, you will likely need to take a safety course and get a hunting license in your state. This is an official piece of paper that proves you know safety laws and other important information. Some states require hunters to display their license on a jacket, but not all states do. Many states also have age requirements for hunting.

Next, practice your shooting before the hunting season begins. Many sporting clubs have shooting ranges. There, you can practice shooting from different positions.

KNOW THE FACTS!

A hunting safety course will teach you to know your weapon and shoot safely. You will also learn **responsible** handling of animals, hunting laws, and first aid.

Shooting practice improves your aim and makes you a better hunter.

25

GOT ONE!

Some states only allow each person to kill one deer per season. Other states with larger deer populations allow you to hunt more. When you get a deer, you fill out a form called a tag that gives you the permission, or okay, to kill the deer. Then you put it on your deer.

Finally, you must field dress your deer. When field dressing, you remove the animal's organs so the meat doesn't **spoil**. You'll need a sharp knife, rope, special gloves, and garbage bags.

KNOW THE FACTS!

Gun and hunting laws differ by state. Check with your state's fish and wildlife agency to learn what is allowed where you live.

26

When field dressing, cut carefully to remove the deer's organs, or inside body parts.

ALL IN BALANCE

Killing deer makes some people uncomfortable. However, people have been hunting animals for meat for millions of years. Even in modern times, hunting is an important way to keep an **ecosystem** in balance. When deer populations get too high, they can harm forests or food sources. Deer can also get hit by cars.

Money from hunting licenses goes to groups that help the **environment**. The great majority of hunters respect wildlife and care about nature. Want to join them? Give deer hunting a shot!

KNOW THE FACTS!

Eating the meat is a big benefit of hunting. Venison is a lean meat, which means it has little fat. Many hunters enjoy making venison jerky, steaks, chili, stew, or burgers.

Deer meat is called venison.

GLOSSARY

adjust: to change something in a small way so it works better

camouflage: colors or shapes on clothing that help hunters blend in with their surroundings

challenge: a test of abilities

compound: made up of two or more parts

defense: a feature of a living thing that helps keep it safe

ecosystem: a natural community of life that includes living and nonliving features

environment: the natural world in which a plant or animal lives

responsible: able to be trusted to do what is right or to do the things that are expected or required

spoil: rot

trophy: something you keep to show you were successful in hunting

weapon: something used to cause someone or something injury or death

BOOKS

Coulson, Art. *Trophy Buck*. North Mankato, MN: Capstone, 2022.

Simons, Lisa M. Bolt. *Go Whitetail Deer Hunting!*. North Mankato, MN: Capstone, 2021.

WEBSITES

Deer: Britannica Kids
kids.britannica.com/kids/article/deer/353044
Watch videos and learn fun facts about different kinds of deer.

Eddie Eagle Tree House
eddieeagle.com
The Eddie Eagle GunSafe® program from the National Rifle Association teaches kids important tips about gun safety.

INDEX

blinds, 20

bows, 18

buck, 6, 7

clothing, 4, 12, 23

field dressing, 26, 27

guns, 12, 14, 16, 26

laws, 24, 26

light, 11, 15

meat, 4, 26, 28, 29

mule deer, 8, 9

Native Americans, 4

orange, 12, 13

"points", 6

populations, 26, 28

"racks", 6

safety, 13, 21, 24

senses, 4, 14, 15

stalking, 22, 23

tag, 26

tree stand, 20, 21